CHRISTMAS CAROLS
FOR CATS

JULIE & JOHN HOPE

ILLUSTRATED BY SUE HELLARD

HarperCollins*Publishers*

HarperCollins books may be purchased for educational, business, or
sales promotional use. For information please write:
Special Markets Department, HarperCollins Publishers, Inc.,
10 East 53rd Street, New York, NY 10022.

FIRST EDITION

ISBN 0-06-018647-X

96 97 98 99 00 ❖/RRD-R 10 9 8 7 6 5 4 3 2 1

CONTENTS

THE TWELVE DAYS OF CATMAS
Sing to: *The Twelve Days of Christmas*

On the first day of Catmas there came a gift from me
A tear in your precious settee

On the second day of Catmas there came a gift from me
Two headless mice and a tear in your precious settee

On the third day of Catmas there came a gift from me
Three fur balls
Two headless mice and a tear in your precious settee

On the fourth day of Catmas there came a gift from me
Four feathered birds
Three fur balls
Two headless mice and a tear in your precious settee

On the fifth day of Catmas there came a gift from me
Five fur-ry things
Four feathered birds
Three fur balls
Two headless mice and a tear in your precious settee

8

You've got the idea now? Come sing along...

...Six strays a-spraying...
...Seven trays a-brimming...
...Eight fish heads reeking...
...Nine fleas a-leaping...
...Ten toms a-wailing...
...Eleven kittens mewling...
...Twelve vet bills coming...

WE WISH FOR THE FAM'LY GOLDFISH

Sing to: *We Wish You a Merry Christmas*

We wish for the fam'ly goldfish
Why in bowl and not in our dish?
We wish for the fam'ly goldfish
To bring us good cheer

Of longing we sing for food to appear
We wish for the fam'ly goldfish to bring us good cheer

We long for the hamster squeaking
Along to his house we're sneaking
We long for the hamster squeaking
A snack we revere

In wonder we sing why live food is here
We long for the hamster squeaking a snack we revere

We're sick of the budgie chirping
Let's eat him and all be burping
We're sick of the budgie chirping
Each day of the year

This food that can talk we do not hold dear
We're sick of the budgie chirping each day of the year

WE THREE MOGGIES DEFIANT ARE
Sing to: *We Three Kings of Orient Are*

We three moggies defiant are
Something's wrong the door ain't ajar
This ain't humane, please to explain
'Ceedingly quite bizarre

Refrain: O – flap to hinder flap to fright
Flap to push with all your might
We are freezing, can't be squeezing
Through a door that's rather tight

Flattens fur and pinches the ear
Traps the tail and bangs on my rear
It's not sporty when you're portly
Wish it would disappear

Refrain

Keep on howling someone will come
Door is opening let's have some fun
We're so willing this is thrilling
Through our cat flap we run

Refrain

COLLAR BELLS
Sing to: *Jingle Bells*

Collar bells, collar bells
Scares the birds away
O I hate this stupid thing
It's with me night and day

Refrain: Stalking through the grass
Jingling sound of brass
Caught nothing for a week
Feeling like a freak

Collar pink, collar pink
O I really pray
I can wriggle out of this
The guys all think I'm gay

Refrain

Collar smells, collar smells
Catching all the fleas
Everyone just treats me like
I have a bad disease

Refrain

13

O COME ALL YE WAKEFUL
Sing to: O *Come All Ye Faithful*

O come all ye wakeful
Find a nice location
A warm knee, a settee
Relax in the sun
Sleep on your sweater
Though your coat is better

Refrain: O let us yawn and snore some
Keeping one eye open
O let us yawn and snore some
Ou-r reward

O come and be gracious
Your bed is so spacious
O choose well and snooze well
And don't make a fuss
Sofa and armchair
Cover them with shed hair

Refrain

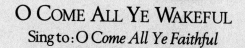

O sleep where you're able
Bookshelf or a table
A good nap on broad lap
Will serve just as well
Life has such meaning
Paws in air and dreaming

Refrain

HOLY FRIGHT
Sing to: *Silent Night*

Holy fright, torment in sight
Great alarm, all's not right
Round the bend to the kennels we ride
Bars on window and nowhere to hide
Sleep without any pe-eace
Weep for early release

Food so bland, trays of sand
No TV, no settee
Fleas all gone and there's nothing to do
No fat mice or a bird I could chew
Sleep without any pe-eace
Weep for early release

Made a pal, O what a gal
She is good for morale
Touching noses there's plenty to say
But tomorrow she's going away
Sleep without any pe-eace
Weep for early release

Nowhere to play, brushed every day
Think I'm going home today
Please come early or walls I will climb
I'll look surly and treat you like slime
Sleep without any pe-eace
Weep for early release

17

THE FIRST SLOW YELL
Sing to: *The First Noël*

The first slow yell for you as you lay
Asleep in the morning on Christmas Day
O do not snore please get out of bed
It's seven o'clock and I haven't been fed

Refrain: O Yell O Yell O Yell O Yell
Feed me at once or I'll make your life hell

To lay a-bed is an awful disgrace
Get up right now or I'll sit on your face
My furry paw 'neath the covers will crawl
Fill up my bowl or I'll caterwaul

Your last big chance now give us a break
I've clawed at your nightshirt you should be awake
I'll niggle and naggle, be ever so rude
For nothing else matters when I want my food

18

O LET US CLOWN AND CAUSE MAYHEM
Sing to: *God Rest Ye Merry Gentlemen*

O let us clown and cause mayhem
Upon you we will prey
To overcome the tedium
We shred your new duvet
Let's rummage in the nice clean clothes
So much to do today

Refrain: O finding some mischief is joy, mischief is joy
O finding some mischief is joy

We overturn the rubbish bin
Across the floor to spread
With dirty paws we wander in
Clean places we must tread
Here's a furball that's a-coming
Leave it on your bed

Refrain

20

O hand us down from this tall tree
We'll cry for all we're worth
The fire engine it will come
As we jump to the earth
Up the curtains we'll be running
There will be much mirth

Refrain

Let's play a game of hide and seek
To find us you must guess
Best humour us before we try
To leave this house a mess
We know you really like the teasing
Come on now confess

Refrain

21

GOOD CLEAN WHISKERS
Sing to: *Good King Wenceslas*

Good clean whiskers wash them out
Comb them straight and even
Face is next now turn about
Back paw, forepaw and then
Lightly on the bit that's white
Shining like a jew-el
Looking good now do it right
Beauty and renew-ew-al

Nap a while then clean a tail
Dry it by the heater
Not too long to make it stale
Smell a little sweeter
Sing a washing song of fish
Birds and hot persu-al
Check reflection in your dish
'Fore it fills with gru-u-el

22

Was it whiskers was it ear
Feel I've done so little
Top of head or fluffy rear
Running short of spittle
Can't remember what I've done
Have a quick review-al
Better start again for fun
Or face ridi-cu-u-le

23

WHILE I DID WASH MY SOCKS
Sing to: *While Shepherds Watched*

While I did wash my socks that night
I quickly looked around
The human of my house crept up
And turned me upside down

Dear cat, said he, O do not dread
We're going to the vet
I'll cry and scream and carry on
And make your car seat wet

It's terrible to wait in line
The place is full of mutts
O awful creature loved by man
Tongues out to lick their butts

Well shocking things did happen there
He held my tail aloft
And squeezed me where I cannot say
Then asked me please to cough!

24

O misery the needle's out
The forepaw he did shave
My claw shot out and he did shout
I showed him who was brave

All glory be we're going home
I'm in an awful mood
I'll turn my back on everyone
And sulk 'til I get food

25

AWAY FROM ALL DANGER
Sing to: *Away in a Manger*

Away from all danger not covered at all
There's sitting a turkey I'm hoping to maul
There's nobody looking, my fate I will seal
And don't you be thinking that guilt I will feel

Now I am so clever I am a good thief
I have to choose quickly 'tween turkey and beef
A fish in a bright dish or cream I will lick
And eat it all quickly until I am sick

I know it's forbidden, I know it's the truth
To eat on the table is really uncouth
But this is so tempting I don't really care
And blame the soft humans for leaving it there

BARK! THE HAIRY SCARY THINGS
Sing to: *Hark! The Herald Angels Sing*

Bark! the hairy scary things
Story of the stress they bring
Fear the feather duster wild
Hate the screaming of that child

Refrain: Bark! the hairy scary things
Story of the stress they bring

Thunder lightning — stay inside
Vacuum cleaners make me hide
Wind in chimney, sirens wail
Slam of door and trapping tail

Refrain

Tripping up when mutts they chase
Jumping wall and losing face
Leaves that jitter, clocks that ding
Horses skitter, kettles sing

Refrain

Funny noises, wind-up mouse
Strangers coming to my house
You must think I'm such a clot
But my nerves are really shot

Refrain

29